REBORN

YOU, YOUR CHILD, AND THE HEART OF BAPTISM

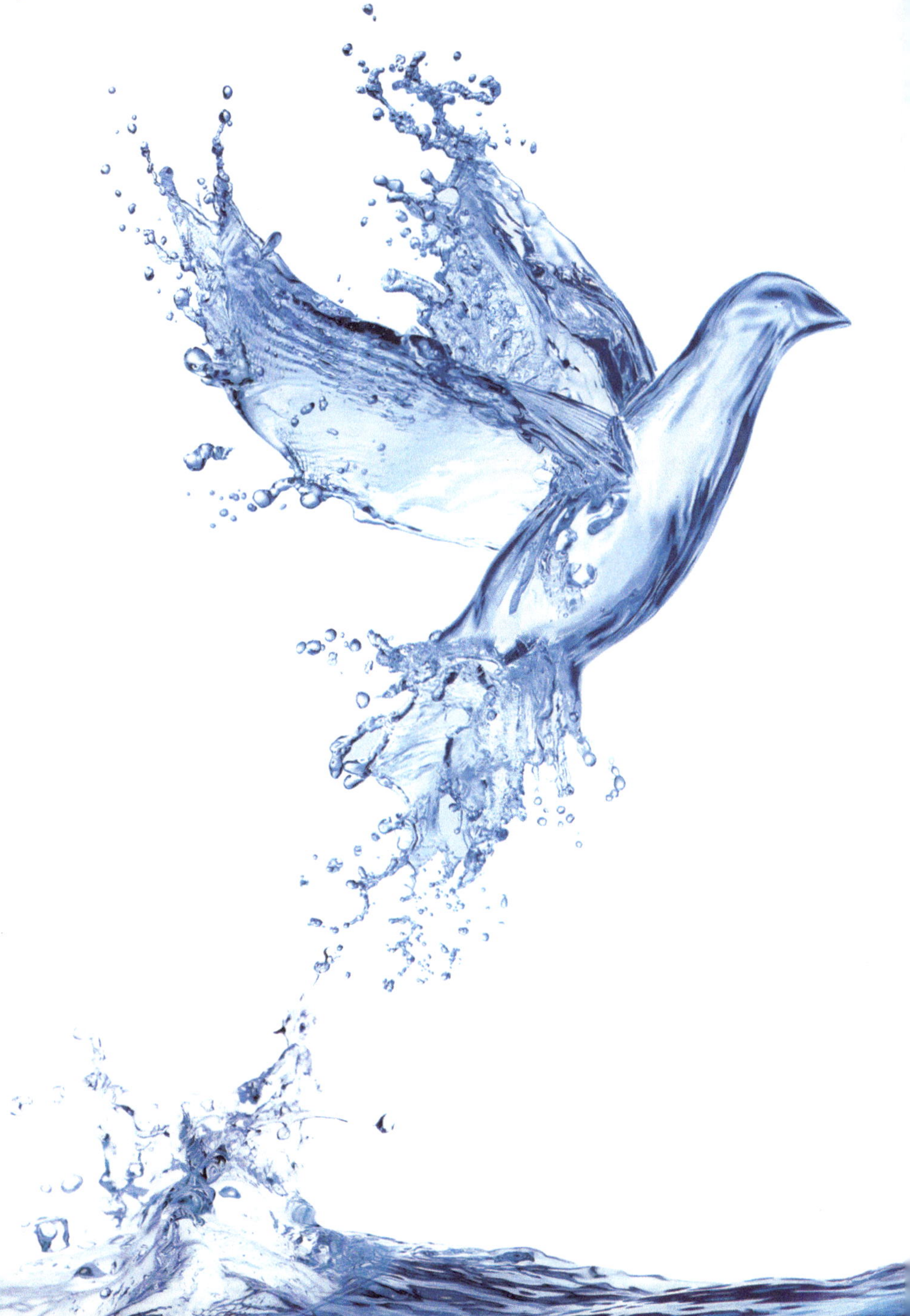

NEW UPDATED VERSION

Leader Guide

Nihil Obstat: Dr. Joseph E. Burns, Ed.D. M.T.S., *Censor Deputatus*
Imprimatur: Most Reverend Samuel J. Aquila, S.T.L., Archbishop of Denver, August, 2015

Copyright © 2015, 2022 Augustine Institute. All rights reserved.

The 2022 edition was updated to reflect the current English translation of the Order of Baptism of Children, obligatory in the United States as of April 12, 2020.

With the exception of short excerpts used in articles and critical reviews, no part of this work may be reproduced, transmitted, or stored in any form whatsoever, printed or electronic, without the prior permission of the publisher.

The English translation of The Order of Baptism of Children © 2017, International Commission on English in the Liturgy Corporation (ICEL); the English translation of Psalm Responses, Alleluia Verses, and Conclusions to the Readings from the Lectionary for Mass © 1969, 1981, 1997, ICEL; excerpts from the English translation of The Roman Missal © 2010, ICEL; excerpts from the English translation of The Order of Confirmation © 2013, ICEL. All rights reserved.

Some Scripture verses contained herein are from the Catholic Edition of the Revised Standard Version of the Bible, copyright ©1965, 1966 by the Division of Christian Educators of the National Council of the Churches of Christ in the United States of America. Used by permission. All rights reserved.

English translation of the *Catechism of the Catholic Church* for the United States of America, copyright ©1994, United States Catholic Conference, Inc.—Libreria Editrice Vaticana. English translation of the *Catechism of the Catholic Church*: "Modifications" from the Editio Typica copyright ©1997, United States Catholic Conference, Inc.—Libreria Editrice Vaticana.

Excerpts from the documents of Vatican Council II are from the Vatican's website (Vatican.va).

Writers: Ashley Crane, Lucas Pollice
Media: Jon Ervin, Steve Flanigan, Justin Leddick, Kevin Mallory, Ted Mast, John Schmidt

Print Production/Graphic Design: Ann Diaz, Brenda Kraft, Jane Myers, Devin Schadt

ACKNOWLEDGMENTS

Our Sunday Visitor

Production of this project was made possible with the generous support of the *Our Sunday Visitor Institute*.

Augustine Institute
6160 South Syracuse Way, Suite 310
Greenwood Village, CO 80111
Information: 303-937-4420
Formed.org

Printed in the United States of America
ISBN 978-0-9966768-0-9

TABLE OF CONTENTS

Overview Program 1

Session 1: A New Creation 7

Session 2: Entering the Mystery: The Rite Explained 17

Session 3: Nurturing the Life of Grace 27

> Let us invoke the mercy of our Lord Jesus Christ for these children about to receive the grace of Baptism, and for their parents, godparents, and all the baptized. Give these children new birth in Baptism through the radiant divine mystery of your Death and Resurrection, and join them to your holy Church. Make them faithful disciples and witnesses to your Gospel through Baptism and Confirmation. Lead them through holiness of life to the joys of the heavenly Kingdom.
>
> —*Order of Baptism of Children* 47

NOTES

REBORN: BAPTISM

AN OVERVIEW

Welcome to the REBORN program. These sessions have been carefully designed to help parents and godparents explore the Sacrament of Baptism's profound effects as they prepare for their child's or godchild's entrance into the Church of God and its sacramental life and mission.

Participants will examine the essential role of Baptism in God's plan for salvation, prefigured from the very beginning of creation and fulfilled in Jesus' own baptism by John in the Jordan. They will discover the real, life-changing effects of Baptism, the beauty of the rite of Baptism, and the mission of Christ which all the baptized share.

The *REBORN* series utilizes three components—this Leader Guide, the Participant Guide, and session videos—to communicate its message. All three are designed to complement one another to educate and encourage parents and godparents.

HOW THE *REBORN* PROGRAM WORKS

The *REBORN* program is divided into three sessions: *A New Creation*; *Entering the Mystery: The Rite Explained*; and *Nurturing the Life of Grace*.

- *A New Creation* traces the theme of baptism through the Scriptures and demonstrates how the Sacrament of Baptism is an essential part of God's plan for salvation.
- *Entering the Mystery: The Rite Explained* answers the question, "Why does the Church baptize infants?" and explores the prayers and symbolism of the rite of Baptism.
- *Nurturing the Life of Grace* examines the call of the baptized to participate in Christ's mission as Priest, Prophet, and King and the responsibilities of the parents and godparents in helping the baptized to answer that call.

The program is structured such that the three sessions may be completed over the course of three separate meetings or together at one longer (half-day) seminar.

LEADING A *REBORN* SESSION

The Leader Guide

This guide takes the leader through the step-by-step process for each session. The various sections are carefully crafted to equip the leader to lead participants through an opening of their hearts and minds to God's Word and the teachings of the Catholic Church regarding Baptism.

WHAT YOU'LL FIND IN EACH *REBORN* SESSION:

1. **Background Info for the Leader:** An overview of the session gives the leader a simple theological summary of the content that will be presented and provides context for the topic.

2. **Lesson Objectives:** The objectives clearly indicate what the participants should take away from each session.

3. **Opening Prayer:** The prayer is included in both the Leader Guide and the Participant Guide. Invite participants to read along silently or aloud.

4. **Introduction of the Lesson:** The introduction clearly and concisely covers the main points of the session, giving participants a sense of what they'll experience.

5. **Video:** The video episode teaches the subject using Sacred Scripture and Sacred Tradition of the Catholic Church as well as by sharing stories and testimonials from parents. The Leader Guide and Participant Guide both include a brief outline that follows the key points in the teaching.

6. **Small Group Discussion:** These questions help participants reflect on the topics of the session together. If you have a large group, consider forming smaller groups for the discussion, with team members facilitating and keeping each small group on track. Encourage each child's parents and godparents to stay together in the same small group.

   We have included possible responses for the Small Group Discussion questions in this Leader Guide. Use these to help get a discussion started, bring greater clarity to the study topic, or answer a difficult question.

7. **Flying Higher:** Both the Leader Guide and the Participant Guide include quotations or excerpts from the *Catechism of the Catholic Church**, writings of the saints, and other Catholic works to help further understanding of a particular topic.

8. **Parent/Godparent Promise:** Parents and godparents are guided through a brief reflection on the rite of Baptism, helping them to more deeply understand their specific roles, while also calling them to a deeper conversion to Christ and the Church.

9. **Wrap-Up:** The Wrap-Up summarizes the key points of the session.

10. **Closing Prayer:** The prayer is included in both the Leader Guide and the Participant Guide. Invite participants to read along silently or aloud.

11. **For Further Study:** Each session includes suggested resources that may be of interest to both participants and leaders for continued study and reflection.

---

* References to the *Catechism of the Catholic Church* will use the abbreviation *CCC* followed by the corresponding paragraph number.

The Participant Guide

This study includes a Participant Guide that contains all of the information that a parent or godparent would need to fruitfully participate in each session. The Participant Guide includes a brief introduction to each session, the opening prayer, an outline of the video, the small group discussion questions, the Flying Higher quotes, the parent/godparent promise and questions for reflection, and the closing prayer. For this study to have the greatest possible impact, each person should have a Participant Guide (rather than parents or godparents sharing as a couple), because many of the discussions require individuals to first journal their thoughts before sharing their responses; it also allows for more personal reflection on the parent/godparent promise.

HOW TO LEAD SMALL GROUPS

The success of any small group begins with an engaged leader. Leading a small group discussion does not mean you have to lecture or teach. A successful small group leader facilitates, getting group participants to interact with each other as they make new discoveries. Here are some tips to help you get started as you lead and facilitate your small group:

- **Set the Tone:** Let group members know from the beginning that your time together is meant to be for discussion and discovery, not lecture. Also remind participants that every question and answer is welcomed and worthy of discussion.

- **Encourage Involvement:** Work to invite all participants to engage in discussion. Don't be afraid of periods of silence, especially during the first part of the meeting. If one person gets off track, kindly acknowledge the person and invite him or her to explore that topic more after your group time. Ask questions such as "What do the rest of you think?" or "Anyone else?" to encourage several people to respond.

- **Open-Ended Questions:** Use questions that invite thought-provoking answers rather than "yes/no" or a one-word, fill-in-the-blank answer. As a leader, your job is to get people to think about the topic and how the Scriptures and reflections can be relevant and applicable to their lives and their responsibilities in the sacrament.

- **Affirm Answers:** People are often reluctant to speak up for fear of saying something wrong or giving an incorrect answer. Affirm every participant by saying things such as "Great idea," "I hadn't thought of that before," or "That's an insightful response." These types of phrases communicate that you value everyone's comments and opinions.

- **Avoid Giving Advice:** Remember, you're acting as a facilitator—not a college professor or counselor. Instead of giving advice or lecturing, when appropriate, offer how a Scripture passage or something in the video spoke to you personally, or give an example of how you've been able to apply a specific concept in your own life.

- ***Be Flexible and Real:*** Sometimes your group time may veer off-track due to something that's going on in our culture or your community (for example, a natural disaster strikes your area or a group member is experiencing a family tragedy). Use relevant topics as a time to remind participants that God is always with us and that we can seek guidance from Scripture, from the Church's teachings, and from the Holy Spirit in every situation. If you model relevant discussion and transparency, your group participants are more likely to do the same.

- ***Stick Around After the Meeting:*** As the leader, make yourself available after your meeting time for questions, concerns, or further discussion on a topic that a participant may have been hesitant about during the scheduled time. If a question arises that has you stumped, admit that you don't have the answer and offer to contact someone who may be able to provide one, such as your parish priest, church deacon, or your diocese.

THREE SEPARATE MEETINGS OPTION

Below is the suggested outline for an individual session when using *REBORN* for three separate 90-minute meetings.

Use the time allotments as a guideline; the length of time spent on each step will vary from group to group and from one session to the next.

TIME	STEPS	OVERVIEW
5 minutes	Opening Prayer/ Introduction	Begin with the Opening Prayer; then go through the Introduction of the session.
30 minutes	Video	Play the video episode.
20 minutes	Small Group Discussion	Facilitate discussion of the questions in small groups.
10 minutes	Break	
20 minutes	Parent and Godparent Promise	Facilitate discussion of application questions for couples.
5 minutes	Wrap-Up and Closing Prayer	End with the Closing Prayer.

HALF-DAY OPTION

REBORN can also be completed in a single half-day event. Here's an example of how you might schedule all three sessions:

8:30 a.m.	Registration/Gathering/Introductions
9:00 to 10:00 a.m.	Session 1
BREAK	
10:15 to 11:15 a.m.	Session 2
BREAK	
11:30 a.m. to 12:30 p.m.	Session 3

For each 60-minute session, use the suggested format below:

TIME	STEPS	OVERVIEW
5 minutes	Opening Prayer/Introduction	Begin with the Opening Prayer; then go through the Introduction of the session.
30 minutes	Video	Play the video episode.
10 minutes	Small Group Discussion	Facilitate discussion of the questions in small groups.
10 minutes	Parent and Godparent Promise	Facilitate discussion of application questions for couples.
5 minutes	Wrap-Up and Closing Prayer	End with the Closing Prayer.

NOTES

A NEW CREATION

SESSION OVERVIEW

 LEADER: READ THIS OVERVIEW IN ADVANCE TO FAMILIARIZE YOURSELF WITH THE SESSION.

This session illustrates how the Sacrament of Baptism is not an empty ritual or mere symbol, but rather an essential part of God's plan of salvation for all mankind. Baptism is a sacrament—a visible sign which imparts grace. Through it we enter the family of God, the Church, and are purified from our sins and reborn in the Holy Spirit. Baptism confers an indelible seal on the new Christian, marking him or her as belonging to Christ, and it can be neither reversed nor repeated. Nothing can remove the mark of Baptism.

To better understand Baptism, we must go all the way back to creation. From the very first verses of Scripture, water is presented as a life-giving part of God's activity. The disobedience, or sin, of Adam and Eve in the Garden of Eden introduces death to mankind and the world. Adam and Eve lose their supernatural life, their union with God, and are marked by their sin; the effect of this "original sin" is passed onto every human to follow. We are, in essence, born to die—both physically and spiritually. The story could have ended there, but Scripture shows us how God began working to bring all of humanity back into union with him—back to life, spiritually. Baptism is a vital component of how God does this.

Baptism is prefigured in the flood, which washes the earth clean for Noah and his family to make a fresh start. The crossing of the Red Sea in Israel's exodus from Egypt is the greatest foreshadowing of Baptism in the Old Testament: Israel passes from slavery to freedom through the waters of the sea, just as the Christian passes from slavery to sin into new life in Christ in the waters of Baptism. Baptism is also prefigured in Israel's crossing of the Jordan River at the end of the forty years in the desert. In passing through the waters of the Jordan, Israel enters into her inheritance: the Promised Land. The waters of Baptism open up the way for the Christian to receive the promised inheritance of eternal life.

The foreshadowing of the Old Testament is fulfilled when Jesus is baptized by John in the Jordan River. By submitting to the baptism of John, even though he was without sin, Jesus set the example for the Church. When Christ descended into the waters of the Jordan, he blessed the waters of Baptism and identified himself with fallen humankind to redeem us.

The Holy Spirit descended upon Jesus and proclaimed his identity for all to hear: "This is my beloved Son, with whom I am well pleased" (Matthew 3:17). Just as the sonship of Jesus was revealed, so our Baptism makes us sons and daughters of God.

SESSION 1 | A NEW CREATION

SESSION OBJECTIVES

- Recognize that the Sacrament of Baptism is more than just a symbol or ancient tradition—it is an essential part of God's plan for salvation

- Understand the Old Testament background for the Sacrament of Baptism and how the Old Testament types reach fulfillment in Christ's baptism in the Jordan

- Appreciate that our Baptism is a participation in both the death and resurrection of Christ

The Baptism of Christ / Digital Image © 2015 Museum Associates / LACMA. Licensed by Art Resource, NY

STEP 1 OPENING PRAYER

▶ LEADER: BEGIN THIS SESSION BY LEADING THE OPENING PRAYER, WHICH IS ALSO FOUND IN THE PARTICIPANT GUIDE, ON PAGE 6.

"O God, whose Son, baptized by John in the waters of the Jordan, was anointed with the Holy Spirit, and, as he hung upon the Cross, gave forth water from his side along with blood, and after his Resurrection, commanded his disciples: 'Go forth, teach all nations, baptizing them in the name of the Father and of the Son and of the Holy Spirit,' look now, we pray, upon the face of your Church and graciously unseal for her the fountain of Baptism. May this water receive by the Holy Spirit the grace of your Only Begotten Son, so that human nature, created in your image and washed clean through the Sacrament of Baptism from all the squalor of the life of old, may be found worthy to rise to the life of newborn children through water and the Holy Spirit."

— Blessing of Water and Invocation of God over Water, *Order of Baptism of Children* 91

Heavenly Father, we thank you for the cleansing waters of Baptism. In this sacrament we are initiated into the story of salvation and we are sealed as your children. May we always cherish the precious gift of your grace and our place in your plan of salvation.
We ask this through Jesus Christ our Lord. Amen.

9

STEP 2: INTRODUCTION OF THE SESSION

▶ LEADER: READ ALOUD OR PUT INTO YOUR OWN WORDS THE FOLLOWING INTRODUCTION, WHICH IS ALSO INCLUDED IN THE PARTICIPANT GUIDE.

If you made a list of the most important moments and experiences in your life so far, what would you include? Maybe key events like graduations, places you've been, people you've met, new jobs, getting married, or the birth of a child, etc. Few of us would think to include our birth—though obviously without that crucial moment, nothing else could follow.

What about your *spiritual* birth? In the Gospel of John, Jesus tells Nicodemus, "Truly, truly, I say to you, unless one is born anew, he cannot see the kingdom of God" (John 3:3). Your spiritual birth happens in the Sacrament of Baptism, which is the first sacrament a Christian receives. It is the access point for our new life in Christ, the other sacraments, and for the kingdom of God.

> "Holy Baptism is the basis of the whole Christian life, the gateway to life in the Spirit (vitae spiritualis ianua), and the door which gives access to the other sacraments. Through Baptism we are freed from sin and reborn as sons of God; we become members of Christ, are incorporated into the Church and made sharers in her mission: 'Baptism is the sacrament of regeneration through water and in the word.'"
> —CCC 1213

In this first session we will introduce the monumental significance of Baptism, the first of the seven sacraments of the Catholic Church. The *Catechism* tells us that "the sacraments confer the grace that they signify" (*CCC* 1127). This means that Baptism is not just a symbol of cleansing and rebirth; it actually bestows those graces on the one being baptized. This session will walk us through the story of salvation history to show how Baptism was foreshadowed in the Old Testament. New creation, cleansing from sin, a fresh start, freedom from slavery—each of these facets of Baptism is prefigured in the Old Testament.

FLYING HIGHER

"Baptism is birth into the new life in Christ. In accordance with the Lord's will, it is necessary for salvation, as is the Church herself, which we enter by Baptism." — CCC 1277

SESSION 1 | **A NEW CREATION**

 **VIDEO**

 LEADER: INTRODUCE AND SHOW THE VIDEO FOR EPISODE 1, WHICH WILL LAST ABOUT 39 MINUTES, THEN DISCUSS THE QUESTIONS IN STEP 4.

Most of us think of Baptism as something that began with Jesus and the Early Church. Is that accurate? What if the importance of Baptism can be found *before* Jesus' baptism? Let's watch to find out…

VIDEO OUTLINE— A NEW CREATION

I. **To understand Baptism we have to start at the beginning of Scripture**

   A. Creation starts with the Holy Spirit moving over the water—connection between life-giving water and the Holy Spirit, the giver of life

   B. Adam and Eve's sin brings death into the story—Original Sin means we are born without supernatural life

   C. The story of salvation is the story of everything God does to bring his people back into union with him

   D. God uses water to give humanity a fresh start with Noah and his family

   E. Moses is drawn from the waters of the Nile as an infant, and God draws Israel out of slavery in Egypt through the waters of the Red Sea—this is a type of Baptism (CCC 1221)

   F. Ezekiel 36:25–26: "I will sprinkle clean water upon you, and you shall be clean from all your uncleannesses, and from all your idols I will cleanse you. A new heart I will give you, and a new spirit I will put within you."

   G. John the Baptist's baptism of repentance— Jesus makes the waters holy

   H. Jesus sees his crucifixion as a kind of baptism—Saint Paul sees our Baptism as a participation in Christ's death and resurrection

II. **Baptism is an essential part of God's plan to save us**

   A. Baptism is a visible action with an invisible power, meaning, and grace

   B. Baptism is not just an ancient symbol but it frees us from sin and makes us a new creation in Christ

11

 SMALL GROUP DISCUSSION

> LEADER: PARENTS SHOULD BE SEATED WITH THEIR CHILD'S GODPARENTS.
>
> READ THE FOLLOWING QUESTIONS ALOUD ONE AT A TIME, GIVING THE SMALL GROUPS TIME TO ANSWER EACH ONE. REFER TO THE RESPONSE IN ITALICS BELOW EACH QUESTION AS NEEDED TO HELP FACILITATE CONVERSATION. ANSWERS WILL, OF COURSE, VARY.
>
> KEEP A BRISK PACING FOR THESE DISCUSSIONS (MOVING ALONG, BUT NOT RUSHED). WHEN YOU NOTICE THE DISCUSSION OF ONE QUESTION WRAPPING UP, MOVE ON TO THE NEXT ONE.

1. **Have you ever attended a Baptism? What details do you remember about the Baptism?**

   Personal responses.

2. **Which type (prefigurement) of baptism in the Old Testament caught your attention the most? Why? Did any of those types of Baptism come as a surprise to you? Explain?**

   A particular type of baptism may have caught a participant's attention because it was new to them, or because that Old Testament story already holds a special significance. Types of baptism found in the Old Testament include: the creation (where the Spirit moves over the face of the water, new life coming out of the water, and where a river runs through the Garden of Eden bringing life), the flood (where water brings death to sin, and where there is a newness of life after the water of the flood), the Exodus (where freedom from slavery comes after passing through the water of the Red Sea and then begins a journey to the Promised Land), etc.

3. **Ezekiel 36:25–26 says, "I will sprinkle clean water upon you, and you shall be clean from all your uncleannesses, and from all your idols I will cleanse you. A new heart I will give you, and a new spirit I will put within you." What do you think it means to have a new heart and a new spirit through Baptism?**

   The baptized Christian is a new creation. He or she belongs to Christ and has received the Holy Spirit. The heart is new because it is washed clean of sin; the spirit is new because the Spirit of God now dwells with the Christian.

4. **Why do you desire Baptism for your child or godchild? What is your deepest desire for your child or godchild in Baptism?**

   Personal responses. Some may desire Baptism because they want the sacramental grace for their child. Some may not understand the deeper significance yet but see it as an important tradition to keep.

FLYING HIGHER

"Baptism is God's most beautiful and magnificent gift… We call it gift, grace, anointing, enlightenment, garment of immortality, bath of rebirth, seal, and most precious gift. It is called gift because it is conferred on those who bring nothing of their own; grace since it is given even to the guilty; Baptism because sin is buried in the water; anointing for it is priestly and royal as are those who are anointed; enlightenment because it radiates light; clothing since it veils our shame; bath because it washes; and seal as it is our guard and the sign of God's Lordship." —Saint Gregory of Nazianzus

SESSION 1 | A NEW CREATION

STEP 5 — PARENT/GODPARENT PROMISE

▶ LEADER: DIRECT THE PARENTS AND GODPARENTS TO THE FOLLOWING REFLECTION QUESTIONS FOUND ON PAGE 9 IN THEIR PARTICIPANT GUIDES.

TO THE PARENT

Just as God saved his people Israel from slavery in Egypt by the waters of the Red Sea, God wants to give your child a life of freedom in him through the waters of Baptism. By seeking Baptism for your child, you are God's instrument leading him or her to freedom and new life, as Moses led the Israelites. It is God who saves, but as a parent choosing Baptism for your child you have a unique and precious role to play, both now and after the Baptism.

Consider the following prayer from the rite of Baptism:
Almighty ever-living God,
who sent your Son into the world
to drive out from us the power of Satan, the spirit of evil,
and bring the human race, rescued from darkness,
into the marvelous Kingdom of your light:
we humbly beseech you
to free this child from Original Sin,
to make him (her) the temple of your glory,
and to grant that your Holy Spirit may dwell in him (her)….
May the strength of Christ the Savior protect you. As a sign of this we anoint you with the oil of salvation in the same Christ our Lord, who lives and reigns for ever and ever. Amen.

—Prayer of Exorcism and Anointing before Baptism, *Order of Baptism of Children* 86–87

Saint Augustine being baptized by Saint Ambrose of Milan / Scala / Art Resource, NY

The prayer describes the spiritual reality of Baptism: freedom from Original Sin and darkness, and freedom to become a temple radiating the light of God's glory. The prayer asks God to strengthen the child for the journey of life that is ahead. You are the first answer to that prayer. You are the first means by which God will protect and guide your child.

What will you do to help your child walk in the freedom of his or her identity as God's child?
How will you help him or her resist the spirit of evil and walk always in the light of God?
How can you start fulfilling this mission even now?

13

TO THE GODPARENT

In the Exodus, God saved his people Israel from slavery in Egypt and brought them to the Promised Land with many signs and wonders. He also used many human leaders to teach and guide his people. Moses led the people and gave them God's law. Moses' brother Aaron led the people in worship as High Priest. Moses' sister Miriam led the people in praising God as a prophetess. At God's command, Moses appointed 70 elders to help him govern the people in the wilderness.

By agreeing to be a godparent, you are answering the call to guide and protect the newly Baptized as God's chosen leaders guided the Israelites when God brought his people from slavery to freedom.

Consider the following prayer from the rite of Baptism:
Almighty ever-living God,
who sent your Son into the world
to drive out from us the power of Satan, the spirit of evil,
and bring the human race, rescued from darkness,
into the marvelous Kingdom of your light:
we humbly beseech you to free this child from Original Sin,
to make him (her) the temple of your glory,
and to grant that your Holy Spirit may dwell in him (her)....
May the strength of Christ the Savior protect you. As a sign of
this we anoint you with the oil of salvation in the same Christ
our Lord, who lives and reigns for ever and ever. Amen.

—Prayer of Exorcism and Anointing before Baptism, *Order of Baptism of Children* 86–87

Although the newly baptized child will immediately enter into the freedom of the sons and daughters of God that freedom is not without challenges and temptations. It is your mission as godparent to be an instrument of God in strengthening and supporting your godchild, watching over him or her at every step in life's journey.

What will you do to help your godchild walk in the freedom of his or her identity as God's child? How will you help him or her resist the spirit of evil and walk always in the light of God? How can you start fulfilling this mission even now?

FLYING HIGHER

"Baptism not only purifies from all sins, but also makes the neophyte 'a new creature,' an adopted son of God, who has become a 'partaker of the divine nature,' member of Christ and co-heir with him, and a temple of the Holy Spirit." —CCC 1265

SESSION 1 | **A NEW CREATION**

 # WRAP-UP & CLOSING PRAYER

▶ LEADER: REVIEW THE KEY POINTS OF THIS SESSION TOGETHER. PARTICIPANTS SHOULD LEAVE THIS SESSION WITH AN UNDERSTANDING OF HOW BAPTISM IS ESSENTIAL TO GOD'S PLAN OF SALVATION: IT REMEDIES THE CONSEQUENCES OF ADAM AND EVEN'S SIN, WHICH WE CALL ORIGINAL SIN—THE LOSS OF SUPERNATURAL LIFE AND UNION WITH GOD—AND MAKES US CHILDREN OF GOD. PARTICIPANTS SHOULD ALSO COME AWAY WITH AN UNDERSTANDING OF HOW CREATION, THE FLOOD, AND THE EXODUS FORESHADOW BAPTISM. FINALLY, PARTICIPANTS SHOULD RECOGNIZE THAT BAPTISM IS A PARTICIPATION IN CHRIST'S DEATH AND RESURRECTION: IN BAPTISM WE DIE TO SIN AND ARE RAISED TO NEW LIFE IN CHRIST.

▶ LEADER: CLOSE THE SESSION WITH PRAYER

> **Lord Jesus Christ,**
> we thank you for the gift of our own Baptism.
> Thank you for the gift of your grace,
> for the forgiveness of our sins,
> and for making us sons and daughters of the Father.
> May we always strive to live fully in the freedom
> you have given us in Baptism,
> to reject sin and evil,
> and to keep our eyes fixed on the hope of eternal life.
> Strengthen us against the temptations
> and difficulties of this journey,
> and help us support and encourage those around us.
> Amen.

FOR FURTHER STUDY

- Benedict XVI. "Chapter One: The Baptism of Jesus" in *Jesus of Nazareth* (San Francisco: Ignatius Press, 2007)
- *Catechism of the Catholic Church* 1217–1228

Saint Ambrose baptizes Saint Augustine / Scala / Art Resource, NY

15

NOTES

SESSION 2

ENTERING THE MYSTERY:
THE RITE EXPLAINED

YOU, YOUR CHILD, AND THE HEART OF BAPTISM

ENTERING THE MYSTERY:
THE RITE EXPLAINED

SESSION OVERVIEW

 LEADER: READ THIS OVERVIEW IN ADVANCE TO FAMILIARIZE YOURSELF WITH THE SESSION.

In the last session we saw how Baptism was prefigured in different events in the Old Testament. This session will continue to explore the importance of Baptism, examine the reasons that the Catholic Church baptizes infants as well as those old enough to consent, and walk through the various parts of the rite of Baptism.

In each type of Baptism found in the Old Testament—creation, the flood, the Exodus—God brought forth new life out of water. These Old Testament events set the precedent for understanding the necessity of Baptism in our salvation. Jesus indicates the importance of Baptism when he submits to the baptism of John and when he commands his disciples not only to preach the Gospel but also to baptize (see Matthew 28:19). The *Catechism* clearly states that Baptism is necessary for salvation "for those to whom the Gospel has been proclaimed and who have had the possibility of asking for this sacrament" (*CCC* 1257), but it also says that "God has bound salvation to the sacrament of Baptism, but he himself is not bound by his sacraments" (*CCC* 1257). Because of this the Church cannot choose to neglect the important mission of Baptism, and we trust those who are ignorant of the Gospel and those who do not have the opportunity to be baptized to the mercy of God (*CCC* 1258–1261).

Because of the importance of Baptism for salvation, the Church does not reserve Baptism only for those who are old enough to choose it for themselves. Just as parents make decisions on behalf of a child to ensure physical and emotional well-being long before the child can consent, parents also make decisions for the sake of their child's spiritual well-being. What parent wouldn't want their child cleansed from Original Sin (and personal sin, in the case of adults and children old enough to have committed sins)? What parent wouldn't want their child restored to a state of innocence and right relationship with God? Baptism accomplishes this. And, through it, God also gives the grace of justification, which bestows on the new Christian the theological virtues of faith, hope, and love (*CCC* 1266). Infant Baptism confers this state of grace and this gift of faith at the very beginning of the child's life.

Infant Baptism also follows an Old Testament precedent. Starting with Abraham's son Isaac, male children were to be circumcised on the eighth day after birth as a sign of their entrance into God's covenant with Israel. Similar to Mary and Joseph bringing Jesus to be circumcised, parents act on behalf of their child to bring the infant into God's family through Baptism at the beginning of the child's life.

SESSION 2 | ENTERING THE MYSTERY: THE RITE EXPLAINED

The rite of Baptism is rich with significance. Each prayer and action points to a different aspect of the meaning and effects of Baptism. The rite itself is a catechesis, explaining and meditating on the beauty of this sacrament. Examining the rite of Baptism helps us to gain a deeper appreciation for what Baptism accomplishes and allows the parents and godparents to have a more fruitful participation in the rite.

SESSION OBJECTIVES

- Understand why Baptism is essential for salvation and understand the effects of Baptism
- Understand that choosing Baptism for an infant is caring for his/her spiritual health, just as parents care for their child's physical and emotional health
- Become familiar with the various parts of the rite of Baptism and what each means

OPENING PRAYER

▶ LEADER: BEGIN THIS SESSION BY LEADING THE OPENING PRAYER, WHICH IS ALSO FOUND IN THE PARTICIPANT GUIDE, ON PAGE 14.

"Receive the light of Christ. Parents and godparents,
this light is entrusted to you to be kept burning brightly,
so that your child, enlightened by Christ,
may walk always as a child of the light
and, persevering in the faith,
may run to meet the Lord when he comes
with all the Saints in the heavenly court."

—Handing On of a Lighted Candle,
Order of Baptism of Children 100

Lord God, you are light, and in you there is no darkness.
In Baptism you give us your light and call us to be light for the world.
Help us to nurture the flame of faith we have received, to walk in
your light, and to guide and encourage our children and godchildren
to grow in your light. May we always live our lives
to give glory to you. We ask this in Jesus' holy name. Amen.

STEP 2 INTRODUCTION OF THE SESSION

▶ LEADER: READ ALOUD OR PUT INTO YOUR OWN WORDS THE FOLLOWING INTRODUCTION, WHICH IS ALSO INCLUDED IN THE PARTICIPANT GUIDE.

As we discussed in the last session, the Sacrament of Baptism is an essential part of God's plan for salvation, actually conferring the grace it signifies. In a society that highly celebrates personal choice, it may come as a surprise that something as important and life-changing as Baptism can be chosen on behalf of an infant; the sacrament is not reserved for consenting adults or children. What is the Church's rationale for baptizing infants?

In this session we will explore the significant signs and symbols in the rite of Baptism in order to understand the vital change effected by this sacrament. It's much more than just pouring water and pronouncing the name of the Trinity.

> "The meaning and grace of the sacrament of Baptism are clearly seen in the rites of its celebration. By following the gestures and words of this celebration with attentive participation, the faithful are initiated into the riches this sacrament signifies and actually brings about in each newly baptized person."
>
> —CCC 1234

FLYING HIGHER

"The custom of Mother Church in baptizing infants is certainly not to be scorned, nor is it to be regarded in any way as superfluous, nor is it to be believed that its tradition is anything except apostolic." —Saint Augustine

SESSION 2 | ENTERING THE MYSTERY: THE RITE EXPLAINED

 VIDEO

 LEADER: INTRODUCE AND SHOW THE VIDEO FOR EPISODE 2, WHICH WILL LAST ABOUT 24 MINUTES. THEN DISCUSS THE QUESTIONS IN STEP 4.

Why does the Church baptize infants? How do the different prayers and actions in the rite of Baptism reveal the deep and beautiful truth of Baptism? Let's watch to find out...

VIDEO OUTLINE— ENTERING THE MYSTERY: THE RITE EXPLAINED

I. **Baptism is necessary for salvation**

    A. New life came by way of water in both creation and the Exodus

    B. Jesus included baptism in his last instructions to his disciples

II. **Just as parents take care of their child's physical well-being without the child's consent, Baptism is an important piece of the child's spiritual well-being, even if the baby can't choose it or consent to it**

    A. Baptism cleanses us from the guilt of Original Sin and frees us from slavery to the power of darkness

    B. Infant Baptism follows the precedent of the Jewish tradition of infant circumcision

    C. Baptism brings us into the family of God

III. **Rite of Baptism**

    A. Introductory Rites

        1. Sign of the Cross—victory of Christ

        2. Reception of the child

    B. Liturgy of the Word—evokes a response of faith

        1. Biblical Readings and Homily

        2. Intercessions

        3. Invocation of the Saints—the child is welcomed into the whole Church, across time and cultures

        4. Prayer of Exorcism

        5. Anointing with Oil of Catechumens—cleansing

    C. Celebration of the Sacrament

        1. Blessing of the Baptismal Water

        2. Renunciation of Sin and Profession of Faith—the parents and godparents renew their vows and take on the responsibility of raising the child in the Faith

        3. Baptism—pouring of water in the name of the Father, and of the Son, and of the Holy Spirit

    D. Explanatory Rites

        1. Anointing with Chrism of salvation—consecration/dedication and gift of the Holy Spirit; sealed=indelibly marked for God

        2. Clothing with a White Garment—symbolizes a pure and unstained soul after Baptism

        3. Handing On of a Lighted Candle—the baptized is now a child of the light

        4. "Ephphatha"—prayer over ears and mouth, to receive God's word and proclaim his praise

    E. Conclusion of the Rite

        1. Our Father—the baptized is now a child of God, and so we pray the prayer our Lord taught us

        2. Blessings for the mother and the father

 # SMALL GROUP DISCUSSION

▶ PARENTS SHOULD BE SEATED WITH THEIR CHILD'S GODPARENTS.

READ THE FOLLOWING QUESTIONS ALOUD ONE AT A TIME, GIVING THE SMALL GROUPS TIME TO ANSWER EACH ONE. REFER TO THE RESPONSE IN ITALICS BELOW EACH QUESTION AS NEEDED TO HELP FACILITATE CONVERSATION. ANSWERS WILL, OF COURSE, VARY.

KEEP A BRISK PACING FOR THESE DISCUSSIONS (MOVING ALONG, BUT NOT RUSHED). WHEN YOU NOTICE THE DISCUSSION OF ONE QUESTION WRAPPING UP, MOVE ON TO THE NEXT ONE.

1. **What are some choices you have already made for your child (or that you have observed parents making for their children)? What would be the potential consequences of delaying these decisions until the child is old enough to make those decisions for him/herself? Why do you think it is important for you to choose Baptism for your child (or to support the parents in choosing for their child)? What are some of the reasons you are choosing Baptism for your child or godchild?**

   Choices may include decisions concerning health, such as vaccinations or treatments for an illness, what clothes to wear, when to bathe, etc. Some of these decisions could be life-or-death matters if the parent didn't make a choice. Baptism is a matter of spiritual life or death, and delaying it until a child can choose it unnecessarily deprives the child of the sacramental grace during the formative years of childhood.

2. **Baptism brings us into the family of God, the Church. This means so much more than just being welcomed into the local parish. The family of God stretches across time and culture. What does it mean to be a part of the family of God? How will you help your child or godchild understand and live out his or her identity as part of the family of God?**

   Being part of the family of God brings a sense of belonging, of identity. It also calls one to a new way of life. It may help bring healing from experiences of a broken human family. Parents and godparents can help the child understand his or her identity and way of life by keeping the child involved in parish life with Sunday Mass and Religious Education classes, teaching the child to pray to God as father, teaching the child about the faith in other times and cultures (especially with stories of the saints), to live according to the commandments of God, etc.

3. **The *Catechism* states, "Incorporated into Christ by Baptism, the person baptized is configured to Christ. Baptism seals the Christian with the indelible spiritual mark (*character*) of his belonging to Christ" (CCC 1272). This indelible seal marks us as belonging to God, and nothing can change or erase the seal of Baptism. What does it mean to be marked as belonging to Christ? Why is it important to you that your child or godchild be marked by this seal now?**

   One possible answer is that being marked as belonging to Christ establishes a two-way relationship: the baptized person belongs to Christ and so must be faithful, but he/she can also depend on Christ's care and protection because of that belonging. Parents and godparents may want this immediately for the child, they may want the child's identity in Christ established as soon as possible, etc..

FLYING HIGHER

"With Baptism we become children of God in his only-begotten Son, Jesus Christ. Rising from the waters of the Baptismal font, every Christian hears again the voice that was once heard on the banks of the Jordan River: 'You are my beloved Son; with you I am well pleased' (Luke 3:22)." —Pope Saint John Paul II, *Chrisitifideles Laici* 11

SESSION 2 | ENTERING THE MYSTERY: THE RITE EXPLAINED

STEP 5 PARENT/GODPARENT PROMISE

 LEADER: DIRECT THE PARENTS AND GODPARENTS TO THE FOLLOWING REFLECTION QUESTIONS FOUND ON PAGE 17 IN THEIR PARTICIPANT'S GUIDES.

TO THE PARENT

The Baptism of your child will be a once-for-all, life-changing event. Studying and prayerfully preparing for this significant occasion is an opportunity to look not only to your child's future as a member of the family of God, but also to reflect on the meaning and effects of your own Baptism.

As a parent choosing Baptism for your child, you will be asked to renew your own baptismal vows. Reflect on the questions from the Renunciation of Sin (Form A) in the rite of Baptism:

> *Do you renounce Satan?*
> *And all his works?*
> *And all his empty show?*

After rejecting sin, you will be asked to make a profession of faith for yourself and your child. Afterwards the priest or deacon says:

> *This is our faith.*
> *This is the faith of the Church.*
> *We are proud to profess it in Christ Jesus our Lord.*

Faith is both communal and individual. As your child grows, he or she will need to develop a unique, individual relationship with Christ and make your faith, the faith of the Church, his or her own personal faith as well. But all of that begins with this decision *you* make for the spiritual well-being of your child. Your faith and commitment now and in the years to come have a very real impact on the fruits that baptismal grace will bear in the life of your child.

Consider the effects of your Baptism and your own life of faith, the faith you will profess at your child's Baptism. What is going well in your spiritual life? Where could you use some improvement to be the best model and guide for your child?

Baptism of Saint Ursula / Scala / Art Resource, NY

TO THE GODPARENT

As a godparent, you are participating in a life-changing event for your godchild. Preparing for this momentous event should include a deepening of your own understanding of Baptism, as well as reflection on the meaning and effects of your own Baptism and the impact you will have on your godchild's future as a member of the family of God.

One way to make your godchild's Baptism real for you is to reflect upon your own baptismal vows as you are asked to renew them in the rite itself:

> *Do you renounce Satan?*
> *And all his works?*
> *And all his empty show?*

After rejecting sin, you will be asked to make a profession of faith along with the parents and the rest of the congregation gathered for the Baptism. Afterward, the priest or deacon says:

> *This is our faith.*
> *This is the faith of the Church.*
> *We are proud to profess it in Christ Jesus our Lord.*

The growth of your godchild will involve both a unique, individual relationship with Christ and a communal relationship with his Church. As a godparent, you are in a special position to nurture those relationships—now and in the years to come. You will have a very real impact on the fruits that the baptismal grace will bear in the life of your godchild. Your prayers and example will play an important part in your godchild's spiritual development.

Consider the effects of your Baptism and your own life of faith, the faith you will profess at your godchild's Baptism. What is going well in your spiritual life? Where could you use some improvement to be the best possible model and guide for your godchild?

FLYING HIGHER

"As we were baptized, so we profess our belief. As we profess our belief, so also we offer praise. As then Baptism has been given us by the Savior, in the name of the Father and of the Son and of the Holy Ghost, so, in accordance with our Baptism, we make the confession of the creed, and our doxology in accordance with our creed." —Saint Basil

SESSION 2 | ENTERING THE MYSTERY: THE RITE EXPLAINED

STEP 6 — WRAP-UP & CLOSING PRAYER

▶ LEADER: REVIEW THE KEY POINTS OF THIS SESSION TOGETHER. PARTICIPANTS SHOULD LEAVE THIS SESSION UNDERSTANDING THE EXPLANATION FOR THE CHURCH'S BAPTISM OF INFANTS AND THE DESCRIPTION AND EXPLANATION OF THE VARIOUS PARTS OF THE RITE OF BAPTISM. PARENTS CHOOSE BAPTISM FOR THEIR INFANTS TO ENSURE THEIR SPIRITUAL WELL-BEING, IN THE SAME WAY THEY MAKE CHOICES FOR THEIR CHILDREN'S PHYSICAL AND EMOTIONAL WELL-BEING. THE PRACTICE HAS ROOTS IN THE OLD COVENANT RITE OF CIRCUMCISION OF BABIES, IS SUPPORTED BY THE NEW TESTAMENT ACCOUNTS OF WHOLE HOUSEHOLDS BEING BAPTIZED TOGETHER, AND HAS ALWAYS BEEN THE PRACTICE OF THE CHURCH. THE ACTIONS AND PRAYERS OF THE RITE OF BAPTISM SHOW THE "MEANING AND GRACE OF THE SACRAMENT" (CCC 1234).

▶ LEADER: CLOSE THE SESSION WITH PRAYER

Heavenly Father,
in Baptism you have made us your own
and marked us with an indelible seal.
May we have the strength and courage
to truly live our lives conformed to Christ,
and to guide those entrusted to us
in the faith of the Church.
We ask this in the name of your Son,
our Lord Jesus Christ. Amen.

FOR FURTHER STUDY

- *Catechism of the Catholic Church*, 1235–1245
- *Instruction on Infant Baptism*, Sacred Congregation for the Doctrine of the Faith, 1980 (https://www.vatican.va/roman_curia/congregations/cfaith/documents/rc_con_cfaith_doc_19801020_pastoralis_actio_en.html)

Sacramentals for infant Baptism in the Church ©
Martin Slanec / shutterstock.com

NOTES

SESSION 3

NURTURING THE LIFE OF GRACE

REBORN® YOU, YOUR CHILD, AND THE HEART OF BAPTISM

NURTURING THE LIFE OF GRACE

SESSION OVERVIEW

 LEADER: READ THIS OVERVIEW IN ADVANCE TO FAMILIARIZE YOURSELF WITH THE SESSION.

The Sacrament of Baptism confers grace and incorporates the new Christian into the mission of Christ. In the previous two sessions we focused on the importance and effects of that grace (cleansing us from sin and making us children of God), looked at reasons for baptizing infants (to care for their spiritual health by making sure they receive this grace earlier rather than later), and examined how grace is communicated through the prayers and symbols of the rite of Baptism.

With the grace of Baptism, we are called and empowered to continue the work of Christ, whose mission was threefold: he was anointed Priest, Prophet, and King. Christ is our eternal high priest, who offered himself as the perfect sacrifice, once for all, to the Father (see Hebrews 7:26–8:2). Jesus is perfect prophet—one who reveals God's Word and plan for salvation—because he is the full revelation of God (see John 1:14, 18). And Jesus is the King of kings and Lord of lords, whose kingdom will never end and will include all nations (see Luke 1:33; Revelation 19:16). In Baptism the new Christian is anointed to share in Christ's threefold mission. The whole community of faith is responsible for helping the newly baptized to live out this mission, but it is primarily the duty and privilege of the parents and godparents to guide the way by word and example.

Baptism makes us a part of the universal priesthood (see 1 Peter 2:5), which is different from the ministerial priesthood—the priests who are ordained. A priest is one who offers sacrifice, and so in the common priesthood of all believers all the baptized are called to offer ourselves daily as a spiritual sacrifice to God. We also offer our worship to God through the Mass, the sacraments, and daily prayer. All the baptized are called to be prophets by sharing the revelation of Christ with the world through evangelization and teaching. And by virtue of our Baptism we are called to reign with Jesus as kings by striving for holiness and mastering the power of sin in our lives, and also by joining our lives to Jesus' mission as servant-King by serving the poor, the vulnerable, and those in need.

The Baptism of Pocahontas at Jamestown, Virginia, 1613 / HIP / Art Resource, NY

SESSION 3 | NURTURING THE LIFE OF GRACE

It's a big job, to model and teach how to share in the threefold mission of Christ. But parents aren't meant to do this alone. Godparents have a real and crucial role to play in the formation of the newly baptized. They are called to help and support the parents, and to represent the whole community of faith in helping and guiding the new Christian.

SESSION OBJECTIVES

- **Recognize that the Christian life is meant to be lived in community, and Baptism initiates us into this community, the Body of Christ, the Church**
- **Understand how Baptism commissions each of us to share in Christ's work as Priest, Prophet, and King**
- **Recognize the role and responsibility of the parents and godparents in leading the newly baptized in the Christian life**

STEP 1 OPENING PRAYER

LEADER: BEGIN THIS SESSION BY LEADING THE OPENING PRAYER, WHICH IS ALSO FOUND IN THE PARTICIPANT GUIDE, ON PAGE 22.

"Almighty God, the Father of our Lord Jesus Christ,
has freed you from sin,
given you a new birth by water and the Holy Spirit,
and joined you to his people.
He now anoints you with the Chrism of salvation,
so that you may remain members of Christ,
Priest, Prophet and King, unto eternal life."

—Anointing after Baptism,
Order of Baptism of Children 98

Heavenly Father, in Baptism you anoint us with the Holy Spirit to participate in Jesus' mission as Priest, Prophet, and King. Grant us the strength and courage to strive to be ever more fully conformed to Christ and his mission, that we may better guide and guard the children you entrust to our care and teaching. We ask this in the name of your Son, our Lord Jesus Christ. Amen.

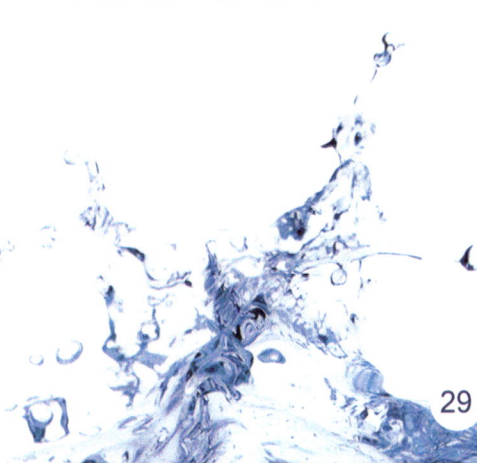

 ## INTRODUCTION OF THE SESSION

 LEADER: READ ALOUD OR PUT INTO YOUR OWN WORDS THE FOLLOWING INTRODUCTION, WHICH IS ALSO INCLUDED IN THE PARTICIPANT GUIDE.

Most organizations have a mission statement of some sort. It helps ensure that everyone is on the same page about the purpose, goals, and identity of the group. The Church, as the Body of Christ, has as her purpose and identity Christ's own mission—and each baptized Christian shares in that mission.

In the last session we explored the reasons that the Church baptizes infants and walked through the various parts and symbols of the rite of Baptism to better understand the grace that this sacrament confers. In this session we will focus on the mission for which that grace prepares us: to share in the work of Jesus Christ as Priest, Prophet, and King. The parents and godparents play the primary roles in helping the newly baptized learn and live out this mission, but the whole family of the Church shares the responsibility of helping the new Christian along the way.

FLYING HIGHER

"Like newborn babes, long for the pure spiritual milk, that by it you may grow up to salvation; for you have tasted the kindness of the Lord. Come to him, to that living stone, rejected by men but in God's sight chosen and precious; and like living stones be yourselves built into a spiritual house, to be a holy priesthood, to offer spiritual sacrifices acceptable to God through Jesus Christ.... But you are a chosen race, a royal priesthood, a holy nation, God's own people, that you may declare the wonderful deeds of him who called you out of darkness into his marvelous light. Once you were no people but now you are God's people; once you had not received mercy but now you have received mercy."

—1 Peter 2:2-5, 9–10

30

SESSION 3 | NURTURING THE LIFE OF GRACE

STEP 3 VIDEO

 LEADER: INTRODUCE AND SHOW THE VIDEO FOR EPISODE 3, WHICH WILL LAST ABOUT 25 MINUTES. THEN DISCUSS THE QUESTIONS IN STEP 4.

As parents and godparents, what is your role and responsibility in helping your child or godchild to grow in the Christian life and share in Christ's mission? Let's watch to find out...

VIDEO OUTLINE— NURTURING THE LIFE OF GRACE

I. **Baptism brings us into the community of faith**
   A. Belonging to Christ means belonging to his Body, the Church
   B. Parents, godparents, and the whole community of faith has a role to play in nurturing the newly baptized

II. **Baptism: Grace and Mission**
   A. Mission of the baptized is to continue the work of Christ as Priest, Prophet, and King
   B. Laity are to bring the Gospel to the ordinary places of life and secular culture
   C. We are empowered and commissioned through Baptism, strengthened in Confirmation, sustained by the sacraments

III. **Priest**
   A. Christ is our eternal high priest—he offered himself as the perfect sacrifice to the Father
   B. Through Baptism we share in Christ's priesthood— the "priesthood of all the believers"
      1. We are called to offer ourselves daily as a spiritual sacrifice to God
      2. We also offer our worship to God through the Mass and sacraments and through daily prayer
   C. Parents are responsible for the spiritual growth of their children—to help them share in the priestly mission of Jesus
      1. Prayer
      2. Reading Scripture
      3. Priority of faith in the family and household

IV. **Prophet**
   A. A prophet reveals God's Word and plan for salvation; Jesus is the full revelation of God
   B. All the baptized are called to evangelize and teach
   C. The power of the Gospel should shine out in family life
   D. Parents are the first proclaimers of the Gospel to their children

V. **King**
   A. We are meant to reign with Jesus over the power of sin in our lives
   B. The kingly mission of the baptized is a universal call to holiness
   C. Christians are meant to govern themselves and reign with Christ over sin in their lives through on-going conversion
   D. Christians are also to exercise their kingly mission by following the example of Jesus as the servant-King who came to serve others
   E. Parents model a life of holiness and service to their children

VI. **Godparents**
   A. Being a godparent is a commitment to active participation in the spiritual growth of the baptized
   B. Requirements
      1. 16 years old or older
      2. A Catholic who has been confirmed and received the Eucharist
      3. Lives a life of faith, in good standing with the Catholic Church
      4. Intends to fulfill the duties of a godparent
   C. Duties
      1. Support the parents
      2. Represent the Church in the life of the child
      3. Nurture the child in faith

VII. **The entire Church is responsible for being part of and nurturing the spiritual life of the newly baptized**

# STEP 4 SMALL GROUP DISCUSSION

 PARENTS SHOULD BE SEATED WITH THEIR CHILD'S GODPARENTS.

READ THE FOLLOWING QUESTIONS ALOUD ONE AT A TIME, GIVING THE SMALL GROUPS TIME TO ANSWER EACH ONE. REFER TO THE RESPONSE IN ITALICS BELOW EACH QUESTION AS NEEDED TO HELP FACILITATE CONVERSATION. ANSWERS WILL, OF COURSE, VARY.

KEEP A BRISK PACING FOR THESE DISCUSSIONS (MOVING ALONG, BUT NOT RUSHED). WHEN YOU NOTICE THE DISCUSSION OF ONE QUESTION WRAPPING UP, MOVE ON TO THE NEXT ONE.

1. **Why is the Christian life meant to be lived out in community? What effect has the community of faith had on you?**
   - *Christian life is meant to be lived in community because God is a community of Persons, and he created mankind to live together in community. There are also practical reasons why the community of faith is important, such as learning from those with more experience and knowledge, having help and encouragement in difficult times, etc. Effects experienced by the participants will vary. Some may feel they haven't received much help or been very included in the community of their local parish. Others will recognize that they only have their faith because others taught, supported, and prayed for them.*

2. **Which aspect of the threefold mission of Priest, Prophet, and King do you think is easiest to live out? Which do you think is hardest? Why?**
   - *Priesthood—offering spiritual sacrifice and prayers—comes easily to some, and feels unnatural or very challenging for others. The mission of prophet—teaching and evangelizing—fits well with some people's gifts for knowledge and teaching, such as speaking in front of groups or talking to strangers, but may be very intimidating to others. The mission of king—conquering evil in our own hearts and living a life of service—may seem to be the most achievable to some, but others may struggle more with habitual sin or pride getting in the way of service.*

3. **Who are the godparents you have chosen for your child? How have they impacted your own faith? How do you see these godparents impacting the faith of your child?**
   - *For many, godparents may be family members, such as aunts or uncles. Others may not know their godparents well because they moved or passed away when the person was younger. Some people have received constant support and encouragement in their faith from their godparents. Others may have godparents who were not active in their lives or have even left the faith. All of these experiences—positive and negative—can guide parents and godparents in their resolution to care for the spiritual well-being of the newly baptized.*

FLYING HIGHER

"The whole Church is a priestly people. Through Baptism all the faithful share in the priesthood of Christ." —CCC 1591

SESSION 3 | NURTURING THE LIFE OF GRACE

# STEP 5 PARENT/GODPARENT PROMISE

 DIRECT THE PARENTS AND GODPARENTS TO THE FOLLOWING REFLECTION QUESTIONS FOUND ON PAGE 25 IN THEIR PARTICIPANT GUIDES.

TO THE PARENT

At his or her Baptism, your child will be anointed with the Holy Spirit and will share in the calling and mission that Christ received: to be Priest, Prophet, and King. As parent, you will be the primary teacher and example for your child in his or her life of faith. It's a daunting task, but you are perfectly equipped for it; you have already received the anointing of the same Spirit and been called into this same mission.

> **Consider the following words from Pope Saint John Paul II in his Apostolic Exhortation to the Lay Members of Christ's Faithful People:**
> A new aspect to the grace and dignity coming from Baptism is here introduced: the lay faithful participate, for their part, in the threefold mission of Christ as Priest, Prophet and King.... Clearly we are the Body of Christ because we are all 'anointed' and in him are 'christs,' that is, 'anointed ones,' as well as Christ himself, 'The Anointed One.' In a certain way, then, it thus happens that with head and body the whole Christ is formed.
>
> — *Christifideles Laici* 14

By virtue of your own Baptism, you are a little "christ," anointed with the same Holy Spirit in whom Jesus accomplished his mission. What your child needs from you is for you to let the Holy Spirit do his work that you may faithfully live out your part of the mission of Christ as Priest, Prophet, and King. It is simple, though not easy. What can you start doing now to live your baptismal mission more faithfully? What can you begin doing as a family now and in the years to come to teach your child about his or her priestly, prophetic, and kingly calling?

The christening of the Princess Royal / HIP / Art Resource, NY

TO THE GODPARENT

At his or her Baptism, your godchild will be anointed with the Holy Spirit and will share in the calling and mission that Christ received: to be Priest, Prophet, and King. As a godparent, your responsibility to set an example of faith and teach your godchild about the Christian life comes second only to that of the parents. It's a daunting task, but you are perfectly equipped for it; you have already received the anointing of the same Holy Spirit and been called into this same mission.

> **Consider the following words from Pope Saint John Paul II in his Apostolic Exhortation to the Lay Members of Christ's Faithful People:**
>
> A new aspect to the grace and dignity coming from Baptism is here introduced: the lay faithful participate, for their part, in the threefold mission of Christ as Priest, Prophet and King.... Clearly we are the Body of Christ because we are all 'anointed' and in him are 'christs,' that is, 'anointed ones,' as well as Christ himself, 'The Anointed One.' In a certain way, then, it thus happens that with head and body the whole Christ is formed.
>
> — *Christifideles Laici* 14

By virtue of your own Baptism, you are a little "christ," anointed with the same Holy Spirit in whom Jesus accomplished his mission. What your godchild needs from you is for you to let the Holy Spirit do his work that you may faithfully live out your part of the mission of Christ as Priest, Prophet, and King. It is simple, though not easy. What can you start doing now to live your baptismal mission more faithfully? What can you begin doing now and in the years to come to support and encourage the parents of your godchild? What can you do to help teach your godchild about his or her priestly, prophetic, and kingly calling?

FLYING HIGHER

"The Second Vatican Council confirmed this tradition in its description of the missionary character of the entire People of God and of the apostolate of the laity in particular, emphasizing the specific contribution to missionary activity which they are called to make.... It is a right and duty based on their baptismal dignity, whereby 'the faithful participate, for their part, in the threefold mission of Christ as Priest, Prophet and King.'"

—Pope Saint John Paul II, *Redemptoris Missio* 71

SESSION 3 | NURTURING THE LIFE OF GRACE

STEP 6 WRAP-UP & CLOSING PRAYER

▶ LEADER: REVIEW THE KEY POINTS OF THIS SESSION TOGETHER. PARTICIPANTS SHOULD UNDERSTAND THAT THE CHRISTIAN LIFE IS MEANT TO BE LIVED IN COMMUNITY—THE CHURCH; THAT BAPTISM COMMISSIONS EACH OF US TO SHARE IN CHRIST'S WORK AS PRIEST, PROPHET, AND KING; AND THAT PARENTS AND GODPARENTS HAVE A UNIQUE AND IRREPLACEABLE ROLE IN SETTING AN EXAMPLE AND TEACHING THE NEWLY BAPTIZED WHAT IT MEANS TO LIVE OUT THIS BAPTISMAL MISSION.

▶ LEADER: CLOSE THE SESSION WITH PRAYER

Almighty God, in Baptism you have poured out
your grace upon us to cleanse us of our sins
and make us your children.
Filled with the Holy Spirit, you call us
to share in the mission of your Son
and live faithfully as members of his Body, the Church.
Help us to encourage one another
as we each offer you our sacrifice of worship,
share your Word and your love with those around us, and
work to conquer sin in our own lives. Amen.

FOR FURTHER STUDY

- *Catechism of the Catholic Church,* 1253–1255, 1267–1274
- Father Robert Barron. *Priest, Prophet, King* (DVD), available from Word on Fire Ministries
- Scott Hahn & Mike Aquilina, "Week 2 with St. Cyril of Jerusalem: On Baptism and Confirmation" in *Living the Mysteries: A Guide for Unfinished Christians* (Huntington, IN: Our Sunday Visitor, 2003)

The Baptism of Saint Cornelius the Centurion / HIP / Art Resource, NY

35

NOTES

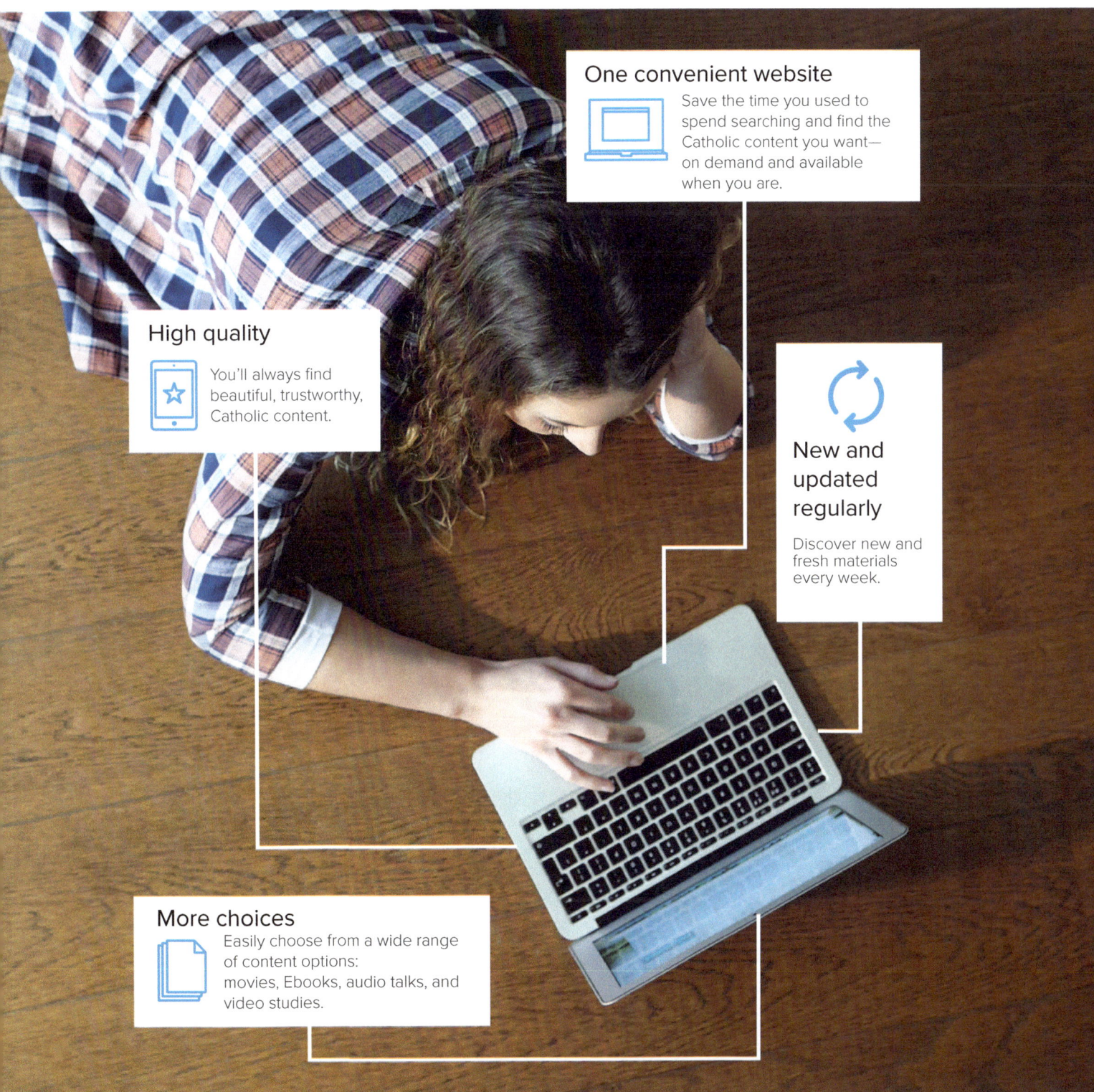

It's not about what it is.
It's about *Who* it is.

Prepare yourself and your family to receive Jesus in the Eucharist as never before with *Presence: The Mystery of the Eucharist*. World-renowned Catholic presenters unveil the truth and beauty behind the "source and summit" of the Christian life, from its origins in Sacred Scripture, to its profound role in the life of the Church and its members.

Learn more at AugustineInstitute.org/Presence

Presence™
THE MYSTERY OF THE EUCHARIST

AUGUSTINE INSTITUTE

TAKING CATHOLIC BIBLE STUDY TO A NEW LEVEL

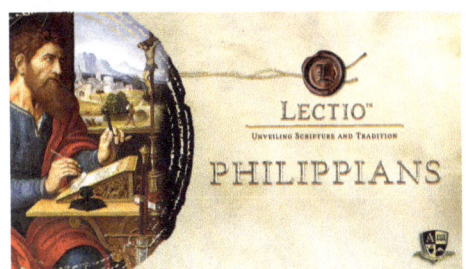  

Compelling Catholic presenters bring together insightful teaching and practical guidance to make Scripture come alive.

AugustineInstitute.org/lectio

FROM THE AUGUSTINE INSTITUTE GRADUATE SCHOOL OF THEOLOGY

Short Courses
Certification and Enrichment for Catholics

Study Catholic theology online. Develop a deeper understanding of your Catholic Faith with engaging curriculum designed and taught by the Augustine Institute faculty. Earn your certificate in Catholic Theology at the conclusion of the nine-course core curriculum. Each Short Course includes

- Three hours of high-quality video instruction
- Detailed companion presentation slides
- Reading assignments that are modest in length but generous in depth and beauty
- Quizzes to guide your learning
- Related resources: books, video, audio, and more

Learn more at
AugustineInstitute.org/ShortCourses